COLOUR THERAPY
—Miracle of Sun Rays

COLOUR THERAPY
—Miracle of Sun Rays

Rashmi Sharma
Spl. in Herbal Beauty Treatments and Naturopathy
&
Maharaj Krishan Sharma
Spl. in Nature Cure, Acupressure, Shiatsu and Reiki

PUSTAK MAHAL®

Publishers
Pustak Mahal®

J-3/16, Daryaganj, New Delhi-110002
☎ 23276539, 23272783, 23272784 • *Fax:* 011-23260518
E-mail: info@pustakmahal.com • *Website:* www.pustakmahal.com

Sales Centre
- 10-B, Netaji Subhash Marg, Daryaganj, New Delhi-110002
  ☎ 23268292, 23268293, 23279900 • *Fax:* 011-23280567
  E-mail: rapidexdelhi@indiatimes.com
- Hind Pustak Bhawan
  6686, Khari Baoli, Delhi-110006
  ☎ 23944314, 23911979

Branches
Bengaluru: ☎ 080-22234025 • *Telefax:* 080-22240209
E-mail: pustak@airtelmail.in • pustak@sancharnet.in
Mumbai: ☎ 022-22010941, 022-22053387
E-mail: rapidex@bom5.vsnl.net.in
Patna: ☎ 0612-3294193 • *Telefax:* 0612-2302719
E-mail: rapidexptn@rediffmail.com
Hyderabad: *Telefax:* 040-24737290
E-mail: pustakmahalhyd@yahoo.co.in

© **Pustak Mahal, New Delhi**

ISBN 978-81-223-0126-7

Edition: 2011

The Copyright of this book, as well as all matter contained herein (including illustrations) rests with the Publishers. No person shall copy the name of the book, its title design, matter and illustrations in any form and in any language, totally or partially or in any distorted form. Anybody doing so shall face legal action and will be responsible for damages.

Printed at : Param Offsetters, Okhla, New Delhi-110020

CONTENTS

Preface vii

Introduction 9

1. **Basics to Science of Colours** 13
   Getting the Feel of Colours 15
   Primary Colours 16

2. **Effects of Colours and Their Characteristics** 17

3. **The Psychological Effects of Colours** 21
   What Your Favourite Colour Says about You 25
   Colour Adoption Associated with Personality Traits 26
   Miscellaneous Effects of Colours 28
   Pull of Colours 28

4. **Healing with Colours** 30
   Radionic Research Using Colour Therapy 31
   Radionic Healing in Action 31

5. **The Basic Postulates of Colour Healing** 33

6. **Ultraviolet Radiation Therapy** 35
   Healing Colours for Certain Dysfunctions 36

7. **Advanced Colour Therapy** 46
   The Principles of Advanced Colour Therapy 47

8. **Colour Breathing** 50
   Procedure for Colour Healing 50
   Treatment Trigger Points for Organs and Body Parts 51
   Trigger Points and Their Treatment 53
   Uses and Benefits of Sun Rays 55

Methods for Application of Sun Rays Therapy 56
Methods for Preparation of Medicines 57
Miracles of Green Radiated Water 58
Dosages of the Prepared Medicines 59
Causes of Illness 60
Treatment of Diseases 62
Properties of Prime Colours 64
Colour-Radiated Medicines 68
Red Colour-Radiated Medicines 74
Orange Colour & Its Properties 76
Orthodox View–A Caution 78

PREFACE

Surya Nivarna is the art of imparting the colour effects of sun rays to different materials. It is not a new discovery of medical science but is thousands years old. This therapy was also used by our ancestors in ancient times. It is part of Ayurvedic treatments. We all know that only with the help of sun rays plants grow, fruits ripe and flowers glow. Different colours of the fruits, flowers and leaves of trees are because of sun rays and property of plants.

Even a layman is well aware of the fact that human beings, plants, flowers, etc. can't survive without sunlight. I have tried to compile my knowledge about the role of colours in treating various diseases in a very simple and understandable way that would enable an average man to comprehend it. I have gone through many old literatures on the science of colours and came to the conclusion that in this computer age the latest costly medical facilities are beyond the reach of average human being who has a shoe-string medical budget. So it is hampering his day-to-day physical conditions and thus leading him towards the jaws of various ailments. It is observed that 95 per cent of various diseases are due to stomach problems. Very few are aware of the ways how to face and prevent them with least efforts and at a very low cost.

My efforts in explaining the methods and remedies as recorded in this book will be rewarded if the readers act on them for betterment of their own health and that of others. The ways explained are so simple that even a layman can follow them to derive maximum benefits.

I am grateful to Ms Nutan, Ms Anjali, Ms Megha for their valuable help and suggestions. I am also thankful to all my colleagues, friends and specially to my kids who inspired me in this venture. I hope my effort will bring coloured fruits for the humanity.

—*Rashmi Sharma*

INTRODUCTION

Sun Rays: Everyone on this earth knows about sun rays and their benefits. It is also not a hidden fact that without sun rays *human beings, plants, flowers, animals* can't survive. The science of colours is age-old, and it is proved by our Shastras.

The sun rays have seven colours those have already been universally accepted and proved by scientists. These are termed in short form as V I B G Y O R, i.e.

1. Violet
2. Indigo
3. Blue
4. Green
5. Yellow
6. Orange
7. Red

According to our Yogashastras, there are seven main chakras in human body. Most knowledgeable persons in India and abroad accept their existence, and the medical science recognises them as glands.

You need to understand that each chakra is related with a particular colour. Each colour vibrates with one or more of the chakra centres. Your body will begin to respond to the colour of the chakra you are developing. If you are attentive to your body's language, you will be able to detect this response.

The first chakra starts from *mooladhara* which signifies red colour and the seventh chakra, beginning at head, signifies violet/blue colour.

It is the duty as well as *dharma* of every human being to keep his body in sound healthy condition. An unhealthy person can't perform his/her day-to-day duties towards his/her family, religion as well as nation. It is must for all of us to be in sound health. For sound health, it is essential to take pure food (*satvic aahar*), pure water and breathe in pollution-free air. Also fill your mind with noble thoughts. Daily meditation is an important means, to keep our mind and physical body in good condition. While taking our routine foods, it should be kept in mind : *what is to be taken, when it is to be taken, and how much is to be taken.*

Good and pure foods, if not taken properly, can't be digested by our body's digestive mechanism. Food should be masticated very well before swallowing. Never be in hurry while taking food. Take ample time to chew the food properly. In other words, *foods are to be drunk and juices are to be eaten.* God has gifted us brain which indicates the fullness of stomach.

One must make it a habit to do *Yoga Asanas* in daily. One should also perform *Pranayam* (deep breathing) with which body remains active and strong. Our goal should be to have a healthy mind in our healthy body. Bowels should be cleaned at regular intervals with the help of *Nauli* and *Kunjal Kirya*. Otherwise, the excreta, if left inside our body, slowly piles up and makes the inside dirty. The accumulated filth causes disease, and illness, and we keep running to doctors and hospitals. Then we have to spend a lot of money and time on our physical ailments.

The medicines are so costly that everybody can't afford to purchase them. In certain diseases some medicines even have to be procured from abroad. Mostly, while taking allopathic medicines to cure our diseases, we have to cope with their adverse side-effects.

Isn't there any cost-effective way of treating diseases through simple medicines? A person who has spent 10 per cent of money on medicines often asks this question.

All those we are tired of taking allopathic medicines, the **colour therapy** provides a better cost-effective alternative. The science of colour therapy is the science of sun rays and is very simple and most beneficial therapy. The sun rays have an abundance of elements favourable for health. To be cured with this therapy you need not spend a lot of money on medicines. You can simply treat your neighbours, friends as well as yourself at a very economical cost.

Since ages, people are worshipping the sun as they know that their very existence is dependable on the sun. The sun is known as a life giver, so it is worshipped like God. And, only because of this reason *shlokas* about the greatness of the sun exist in *Upanishads* and *Shastras. Sun rays have properties and strength to cure many acute/ chronic diseases.* People from Western countries have learnt about the sun rays therapy from the East and practising it for the benefit of mankind.

This book is based on my experiences as well as information collected by other naturopaths on the positive results of the colour therapy.

According to Ayurveda, a disease is caused by disbalancing i.e. excess/deficiency of the following three elementary substances in the human body. These are the microcosmic representatives of the three universal forces:

1. VAYU – Air/Wind
2. PITTA – Bile
3. KAPHA – Phlegm

The primary colours of sun rays are:

1. Green   2. Red   3. Blue

They are available in most of the herbs. However, to practise the colour therapy science you need not trace them or make ash out of them to prepare the Ayurvedic medicine. This simple therapy spares you of all this labour.

It has been observed that this type of treatment is very simple and effective. Even an average person can understand it. The main advantage of this treatment is that you become your own doctor without having any side effects, which most of the patients also realise.

Hospitals are full of patients and the Government is making plans for opening more, but it is beyond their capacity to accommodate each patient and give him suitable treatment. If the organisations working for the welfare of humanity, propagate the colour therapy, they would do a great service to the ordinary people. In fact, colour therapists can treat any disorder, be it mental, emotional, metabolic or physical at a very economical cost. They offer an effective means of promoting well-being which requires no extra money but demands only sustained effort from patients.

✻ Wishing Good and Sound Health for all ✻

1

Basics to Science of Colours

It is an established fact that colours affect on human beings. From time immemorial colours have been symbols of abstract ideas. For instance, Green as in the "Green Pastures" of the twenty-third Psalm, suggests hope or good fortune. Red indicates passion or danger. White in the West is a symbol of innocence and purity. In the Far East, White is a symbol of sadness and mourning. Black, the opposite of White, too denotes these very states in the West. Yellow can stand for cowardice, except in its golden, sunny shades where it denotes power and glory.

Indian medicine is ancient. Its earliest concepts are found in the sacred writings called the Vedas, especially in the passages of the *Atharvaveda* which may possibly date as far back as the second millennium B.C.

In old Vedic writings it has been narrated again and again that the human body is made of *Panch Tatvas* i.e. five elements:

Earth
Water
Fire
Metal
Air

These elements also have their respective colours. Earth is considered as green, Air yellow, Fire red and Water blue.
In feudal times, officials used nine symbolic colours to emblazon armorial bearings.

- Yellow or Gold : Honour and loyalty
- White or Silver : Faith and purity
- Red : Courage, survival & procreation
- Blue : Piety, resolution, creativity and self-expression
- Black : Grief
- Green : Youth, vitality and wisdom
- Purple : High rank
- Orange : Strength and endurance, immunity from diseases and pleasure in life
- Violet : Passion, suffering and psychic awareness.

Inherited

Our endocrine system reacts to a colour in a certain way because of the neurotransmitters we inherited from our parents. Here is how colour plays a role in our hormonal secretions. We see the colour when our brain registers it and sends out a chemical messenger (a neurotransmitter) for a certain hormonal response from the appropriate endocrine gland. An endocrine gland (a ductless gland) manufactures one or more hormones and secretes them directly into the blood stream. They have a powerful influence on human health and well-being. In fact, these minute secretions are produced all along the central body meridian by internal organs and glands which are a part of the body's endocrine system.

The endocrine glands include:

Pituitary
Thyroid
Parathyroid
Adrenal
Ovary (Female)
Testes (Male)
Pineal
Pancreas (Partly)

The endocrine glands react to colours as and when they are acknowledged by the brain. For instance, red colour excites the human brain. Therefore, neurotransmitters stimulate the adrenal glands to pump the adrenaline into the body.

Getting the Feel of Colourts

Sometimes people express themselves in colourful terms. They tell others how they feel by saying, "I am feeling blue" or "I am seeing red" or "I am turning green with envy". Sometimes people say that a certain person is "acting yellow" (as a coward) or "glowing purple with age" or "falling into the blackness of depression" or "rinse in white hope."

Use of the colour to affect or evaluate your own or another person's level of metabolic functioning is called **Colour Therapy**. Health professionals call it as **Chromotherapy**. In brief, chromotherapy is the application of colour for the purpose of healing. In contrast, yellow, green and blue are therapeutic colours. Yellow activates joy. Green is the natural colour of plants. Blue is sedative and pain-relieving.

The first thing the therapist should notice upon entering the patient's room is the environment in which patient is passing his/her whole day (from colour point of view). If it does not have the colour which would help in curing the disease (as will be explained in other chapters), it should be changed according to the requirement of environment colour. This will bring immediate change in the patient's body behaviour.

Colour can be characterised with words that how he/she feels. For strictly descriptive purpose, one could say:

Red   –   Burns
Orange –   Warms
Yellow –   Tepid

Green is natural one and Violet cools the pinching sensation. Orange is an energising colour. Orange and yellow create a laxative effect. They tend to stimulate the elimination of body wastes to such an extent that even the kidneys are cleaned. Thus orange surroundings encourage defecation and urination. You might try orange with your next bout of constipation. *If you have weak kidneys you should avoid citrus juice because it stimulates micturition.*

Different Wavelengths of the Spectral Colours

Colour	Wavelength range (Angstrom)
Violet	4300 – 4600 AU
Blue	4700 – 5000 AU
Green	5000 – 5500 AU
Yellow	5800 – 5900 AU
Orange	5900 – 6000 AU
Red	6000 – 6700 AU

Primary Colours

Red, green and blue are the primary colours of the spectral light because the greatest number of colour combinations can be made from them. Red and green lights, for example, make yellow light. Red, green and blue lights combined in equal amount, produce white light.

Colours can be produced by scattering white light. When white light passes through a medium such as air, it is scattered in all directions by the air particles. The short blue waves are scattered more widely than the longer yellow waves. This is why the sky appears blue. You can show this very easily by an experiment. Take a glass of water and add a few drops of plain milk. Place the glass in a dark room and project a flash light through the water in glass. The light will appear yellow for the blue waves and will be scattered aside. If you look at glass from the side, it will appear blue.

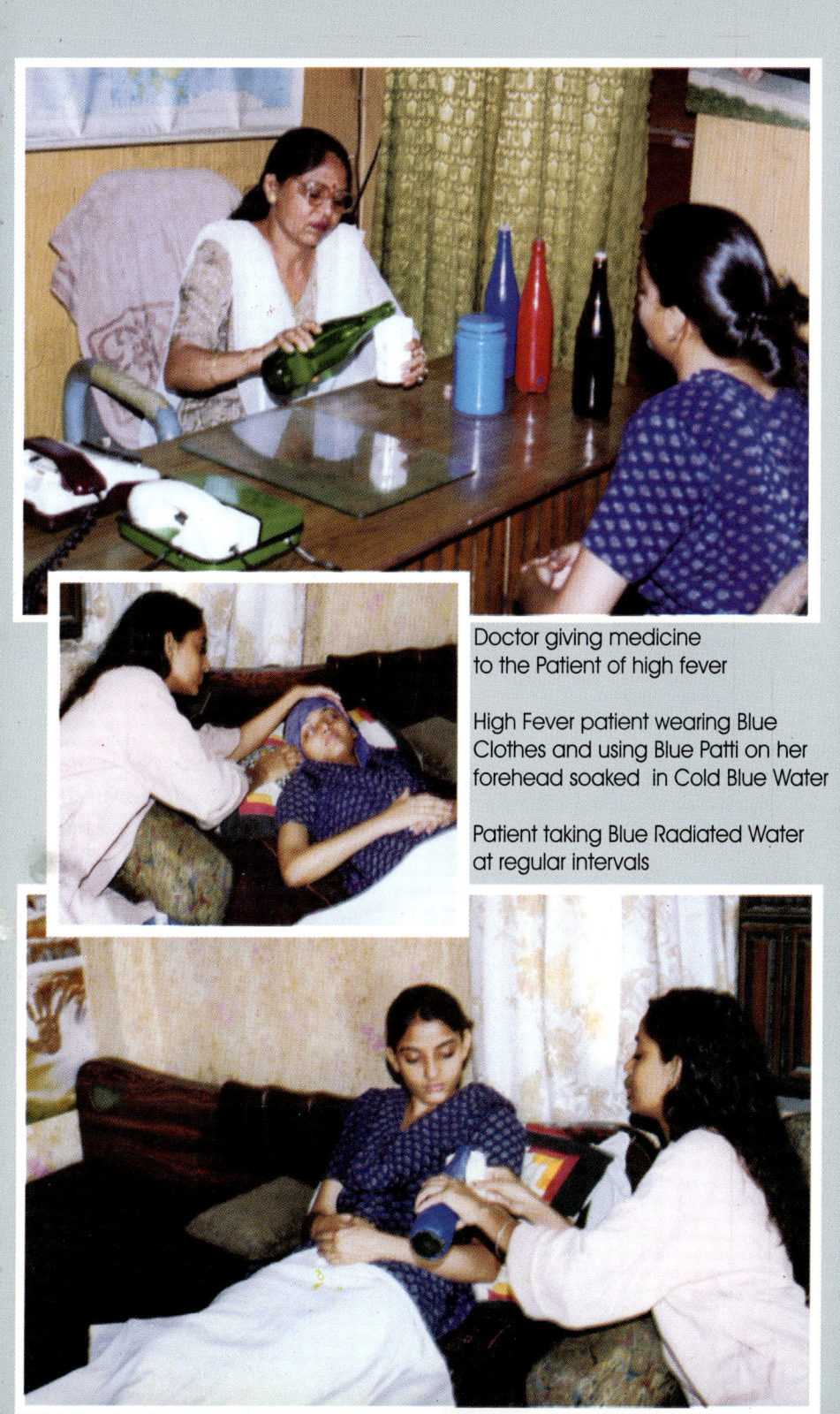

Doctor giving medicine to the Patient of high fever

High Fever patient wearing Blue Clothes and using Blue Patti on her forehead soaked in Cold Blue Water

Patient taking Blue Radiated Water at regular intervals

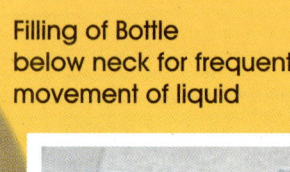

Filling of Bottle below neck for frequent movement of liquid

Preparation of Blue Oil, Blue Misry, Blue Glycerine and Blue Water

Placement of Bottles for preparation of Orange Water

②

Effects of Colours and Their Characteristics

Each colour has its unique characteristics and affects people in a special way. The research on the colours is still going on. The following descriptions focuses on some dominant characteristics of main colours.

Red

Red is the colour that stirs your senses and passions. It is associated with the power, energy, vitality and excitement of life. In its positive aspect, red can stimulate strength, joy, happiness and love. It is one of the primary colours of fire. Deep red (scarlet) can stimulate the animal nature and base physical passions. The crimson of blood represents the suffering elements in life. The gentle pink shade can evoke the mother love vibration. Red is the personal colour of greatest warmth. *The negative aspect of the red vibration can bring out fear, uncontrolled passion, lust and excessive anger. Red can be used when the vitality is low or blood circulation is poor.* This colour is most disturbing to the people with mental problems or neurosis and it should not be used on them. It has the slowest vibrations in comparison to all visible colours. It affects the emotions quicker than any other colour.

Orange

Orange stimulates creativity and ambition along with energetic activity. It can also generate pride and a sense of preservation of self and others. *But excessive exposure to orange can produce great nervousness and restless behaviour.*

Many fruits and vegetables are orange or orange-red in colour, and thus making it a colour of nourishment. Orange represents attraction of elements working as a cohesive atomic force.

Yellow

Yellow is primarily a joyous colour, but it also brings out wisdom, understanding and highest of intuitional insight. In its golden aspect, yellow represents spiritual perfection, peace and rest. It is the colour of sunshine, youth, gladness and merriment. Characteristically, yellow colour makes a dark room brighter where sunlight does not enter. In such a room, cherry colour (bright red) is used as wall colour. It is a good colour to paint the kitchen. Yellow fruits and vegetables tend to act as laxative to the bowel and calm the nerves. In its most positive vibration, golden yellow is deeply spiritual, and brings out compassion and creativity. However, in its negative aspects, yellow, when too bright or used too often, is overstimulating to the psyche and nerves, and can cause mental irritation even to the point of destruction. Yellow in its negative vibrations is also the colour of cowardice, prejudice and destructive domination.

Green

Everybody knows that green is nature's colour. From the pale green of new spring grass and budding leaves to the deep green of the nature's forest, green is soothing, healing, peaceful and cool in its positive aspect. It is a soothing balm for people who are weary in body or mind.

Green has great healing power. On its negative side, green represents selfishness, jealousy and laziness. Heavy dark green can be depressing and even debilitating. Green is useful in soothing pain and calming a teething infant. Yellow Green stimulates generosity on the mental plane and elimination of body wastes on the physical plane. Spring Green represents new life, regeneration, joy and gladness.

Blue

Blue is the colour of heavenly consciousness, truth, harmony, calmness and hope. Sky blue clothing worn by women can bring out the gentle protective nature in the men. Whereas red excites passions, blue soothes and quietens them. The softer hues of blue can sedate the nerves. Blue is a quietening colour and is used in the rooms of violent criminals and mental patients. Soft Blue clothing provides the greatest protection against the sun rays in the tropics. *In its negative aspect, too much blue can be depressing, bringing a feeling of the blues in otherwise healthy people.* Blue and green together can stimulate the highest level of talent and creativity in art and music.

Indigo

Indigo in the spectrum is lodged between blue and violet. In its highest positive vibrations, it combines reason with intuition and discipline with creativity. It simultaneously represents the creative and destructive forces in a person's nature. It also represents the metabolic process in man (catabolism and anabolism) and the divine law of change and growth.

In its negative aspect, indigo stands for stagnation, mental fatigue and starving without success. But it also represents the "breakthrough point" where old failures transmute into new successes, frustrated mental strivings break through to higher consciousness and problems turn into stepping stones to wonderful solutions. Indigo represents the healing crisis of natural art where old toxins and waste are cast out of the body to make room for new issue.

Violet

Violet in its highest vibration represents good motives, elevates spiritual aspirations and enhances consecration of the soul. Violet is associated with prosperity, wealth and increased productivity. Stimulating the spiritual nature of man, the violet vibration offers self mastery, higher realm of creativity and royal consciousness. Violet is the fastest vibration among the rainbow colours, fading quicker than any other colour.

White

White is the vibration of purity and cosmic plane of perfection. It represents harmony in the way it blends all the rainbow colours. The power of white light is intolerable to people who cultivate such base characteristics as malice, jealousy, hate, envy and violence. White light is the great revealer of ultimate truth.

Black

Black represents the absence of light and as a pigment or colour it absorbs the least amount of spectral light. Black, the opposite of white, is the colour of funeral drape and represents the loss and absence of life. Being around black too much can drain a person's health because black absorbs energy and vitality, leaving behind physical and mental fatigue. Black clothing interferes with the proper elimination of toxins through the skin and can bring out a mood of sombreness. The less black clothing a person wears in hot weather the more comfortable he/she will feel.

In its most negative aspect, black is said to encourage the worst in people with criminal tendencies.

Brown

Brown colour in its most positive aspect represents fertility, Mother Earth and the strength of seasoned wood. However, brown is a heavy, severe colour with a slow vibration that also has many negative effects.

Brown should be used sparingly in home decoration and clothing and is best when used with other colours such as white, red, orange and yellow.

In its negative aspect, brown repulses the opposite sex, diminishes personal vitality, negates the life force and implies the decay and dying of nature.

The highest quality of brown colour is that it represents the plane from which beauty comes forth. For example, the mound of the mud from which lily and rose grow. But it reflects no beauty in itself because brown, black and grey (a mixture of white and black) reflect no self beauty. They can be effectively used as a backdrop for a beautiful object, such as a piece of pottery or sculpture. These colours emphasise the beauty of other colours when used as a frame.

The Psychological Effects of Colours

In our routine life, we are always affected and bounded by the existence of colours which have a major effect on our psychology and accordingly affect our body.

Suppose someone is having the blue colour in the environment around him. The existence of this colour is going to affect his strength and aggression. On the other hand, the presence of pink colour has a weakening effect on the physical strength and causes the release of Norepinephrine in the body and brain. Norepinephrine is a chemical that inhibits the specific hormones that contribute to aggressive behaviour.

Physiology studies show that red vibrations increase the blood pressure and elevate palmar conductance. Respiratory movements increase during exposure to red light and decrease during blue illumination. Though heart rate has not shown any appreciable difference in stimulations by red and blue colour, the frequency of eyeblinks increases during exposure to red light and decreases in blue light.

The detailed physiological responses of different colours are as under :

Red

The pituitary gland, which is an endocrine gland, comes into play when a person is exposed to red. In just a fraction of a second, a chemical signal goes from the pituitary gland to the adrenal glands and adrenaline is released. The adrenaline courses through the blood stream and produces certain physiological alterations with metabolic effects. The following reactions begin immediately after a person's exposure to the red colour but may not be noticed for a few minutes or even several hours depending on the effectiveness of an individual's **Homeostasis** (the physiological process by which the internal systems of the body are maintained at equilibrium despite variations in external conditions).

- The blood pressure goes up.
- Blood flow speeds up as manifested by an increased pulse rate.
- The rate of breathing becomes rapid.
- The Autonomic Nervous System takes over and reactions become automatic.
- The taste buds become more sensitive.
- The appetite improves.
- The sense of smell heightens.
- Males become attracted to yellow-based reds while females become attracted to blue-based reds.

Orange

Being half red and half yellow, orange can be either a classifier colour or a declassifier colour depending on the brightness or darkness of its shading.

As a classifier, orange is a pivotal colour for a person making a buying decision. Generally, in the classifying mode, orange appeals to just a limited number of people. As a declassifier, orange moves into another range and appeals to a larger percentage of population making more people to react positively to an orange object or concept.

The physiological effects of orange colour are:

- The appetite elevates and increases.
- Relaxation is induced and the potential for sleep increases.
- The blood flow slows down.
- A sense of placidness, colourness and security develops when orange is combined with blue.

Yellow

As a declassifier with a broad-based appeal, yellow causes the following physiological alterations:

- The electrochemical transference from eye to brain called *Vision* takes place the quickest in the presence of yellow. Yellow is the first colour a person distinguishes when he/she looks on any object. It is also the most complex colour for the brain to process.
- Humans have an inherent precautionary reaction to yellow in nature, especially when it is combined with black.
- Yellow gets a quick though temporary response from a subject under stress.
- Yellow adds to stress by preparing a person for flight to fight.
- Yellow-painted rooms cause children to cry more often.
- Yellow surroundings cause allergies to flare more frequently.

Blue

This colour is known to produce a calming effect. A deep and strong sky-blue colour (known in medical terms as *Cardiac Blue*) is the most tranquillizing colour of all. When it is in a person's field of vision, it causes the brain to secrete eleven neurotransmitters that tranquillize. These hormones are chemical signals which bring calmness to the whole body. They also:

- Slow down the pulse rate.
- Deepen the breathing.
- Reduce the perspiration.
- Lower the body temperature.
- Lessen the sweating.
- Eliminate the flight fight response.
- Reduce the appetite (as very few blue foods exist in nature).

Green

Green is a classifier colour. Forest green, hunter green and similar shades cause an anti-allergic or desensitising reaction in certain people such as those who have "hay fever." In contrast, green with more white and less yellow seems to appeal to a wider percentage of population. Favourable metabolic responses occur inside the body when an individual is surrounded by any shade of green. These sophisticated physiological alterations include:

- Blood histamine levels become elevated. Histamine is a compound found in nearly all the tissues of the body and is associated mainly with dilation of the blood vessels and contraction of smooth muscles such as the lungs. Histamine is a naturally occurring chemical, produced during inflammation and allergic reactions. It is released in large amounts after the skin is damaged, producing a characteristic skin reaction of redness and a weal. Some of the symptoms of the conditions are mentioned below:
    - Allergic reactions to foods are reduced.
    - Sensitivity reactions to monosodiumglutamate are lessened.
    - Histamine release is inhibited from most cells and basophils even when stimulated by antigens and other allergy molecule (ligands).
    - Most cells and basophils are stabilised.
    - Hypersensitivity to food addictives is reduced.
    - Distress from eczema, diarrhoea and gastrointestinal disorders is lessened in severity and duration.
    - Vision chemicals that improve acuteness of sight are produced. The opposite colour of exposed internal body tissue (mostly red) is surgical green, a shade that aids the doctor's eyes by replenishing his vision.

Brown

Brown is generally considered environmentally sound. It offers a healthy encompass or enclosure to work, play, sleep and generally perform common metabolic functions without any hindrance. An aggregate of brown things influence the internal organs and mind in an enhancing way. Brown is a homeostatic colour and lends a sense of security. The presence of brown helps to:

- Dispel mental tension.

- Promote the synthesis of serotonin (a neurotransmitter).
- Reduce irritability.
- Eliminate chronic fatigue.
- Stimulate the formation of prostaglandin E_1. (Prostaglandin is a hormone-like substance in the tissues and the body fluids.) It has many functions and it factors in the actions of the womb, brain, lungs, kidney and semen. Brown effect on prostaglandin E_1 is therefore significant for the body's overall normal functioning.
- Increase tryptophan amino acid levels that influence sleep, migraine, immunity and moods.

What Your Favourite Colour Says About You

When you favour one colour over the other, you are telling a story about your personality and behaviour. For example, a person who dislikes all colours is also likely to hate music, children and the world as a whole. He finds everything wrong with him. Most of all, the colour haters intensely generate negative feelings within them which lead them to frustrations and helplessness.

Colour preferences are innate. You are born with an attraction for particular colours. What you feel about them will probably remain imprinted throughout your life in your mind. *Your colour choice is the result of your genes, early childhood memories, education, parents' beliefs, cultural trainings, political learnings and other aspects of lifestyle.*

Tender children who can't speak whole sentences often express themselves eloquently with a set of crayons. A general delight in colours shown by an adult is considered by psychologists a demonstration of normal emotional tendencies in him. Normally all children love bright colours.

A child's preference for the black crayon probably indicates repressed emotion or strict parental domination. A love of yellow is classified as revealing a youngster's infantile trait and a dependence on adults. Red shows carefree feelings. Green indicates that the child is balanced, with few emotional outbursts and having a simple and uncomplicated nature of mind structure. Youngsters' colour representations of their mothers are always with pastel shades and those of their fathers with darker shades.

And so it is with adults. A preference for one colour over another reveals your true personality—your real characteristics. You then feel and see within yourself through your inner vision. Following are some of the personality traits associated with the colour you adopt as your own.

Colour Adoption Associated With Personality Traits

Red

It shows that you are outgoing. You are assertive, vigorous and prone to impulsive actions and variable moods. You feel deep sympathy for fellow human beings and are easily swayed. You have a strong sex drive, entertain stimulating fantasies and would dive into extramarital affairs if a strong sense of duty did not hold you back from acting on your secret desires. You are an optimist, but you are also a complainer and do not desist to voice your complaints or discomforts.

Orange

You are good natured, enjoy being with other people, and are swayed by outside opinions. You do good work, have strong loyalties, feel good will and possess a solicitous heart. However, unwarranted feelings of elation often pervade your psyche.

Yellow

You have a well functioning imagination, nervous energy, neatly formed thoughts and an urge to help the world. You tend to be aloof and are more aligned to theory than to action. You are inclined to speak of lofty ideas without applying them in practice. Secretly you are shy, long to be respected, crave admiration for your sagacity and are a mental loner. You are a safe friend and a reliable confidant.

Green
You are a good citizen and a pillar of the community and are sensitive to social customs and etiquette. You are frank, moral and reputable. You make yourself a splendid teacher, have a normal sex drive and feel deep affection for your family.

Blue
You are deliberate and introspective. You have conservative convictions and retreat to gentler surroundings in times of stress, but are sensitive to the feelings of others. You keep a tight rein on your passions and enthusiasms, are a loyal friend and lead a sober life. You nourish preposterous dreams but do not act on them. Stupidity in others annoys you as does superior intelligence.

Purple
You have a good mind, a ready wit and an ability to observe things that go unnoticed by others. You are easily incensed and are verbose when witnessing misfortune. You have a degree of vanity. You display a fine arts creativity and relish the subtle but recognise the magnificent.

Brown
You perform your duties conscientiously, are shrewd when it comes to money, obstinate in your habits and convictions. You are parsimonious, dependable and steady. You disdain impulsiveness and can bargain like horse trader.

Grey
You are cautious, try to strike a compromise in most situations. You encounter and seek composure and peace. You try very hard to fit yourself into a mould of your own design.

Black
You are above average, worldly, conventional, proper, polite and regal. Black is a colour that means one thing (depression) to the clinical psychologist and quite another (dignity) to you.

Miscellaneous Effects of Colours

Purple
Diverse interpretations are associated with purple. Purple gives mixed messages. Historically, of course, the purple denoted royalty and grandeur. But this colour is also associated with illness. To symbolise vomiting and other forms of sickness, some people wear a head-band of purple colour.

Red
It increases the appetite. Some expensive restaurants use red tablecloths and napkins to increase the appetite by raising the metabolic rate. People on the weight-control programme i.e. slimming, should stay away from red decorated restaurants, tomato sauce and sliced watermelon.

Blue
People refuse to eat blue-tinted foods. They have a natural aversion to eating something blue. Weight-loss programmes are more successful when foods are eaten while looking at blue decorations.

Yellow
According to latest researches, yellow stimulates anxiety and is the most irritating colour to the retina of people over fifty. It increases blood pressure within thirty seconds.

Black
It brings on a feeling of depression in forty-five seconds. Having the knowledge of these colour effects, we can easily understand how to influence other people. These effects are also used by advertisers, mercantile companies, marketers and industrialists to sway our thinking and buying habits.

Pull of Colours
We are always attracted by the pull of colours which comes under our visibility, like orange draws attention quickly and indicates

informality. It loudly proclaims that the product is suitable for everyone. Orange is a declassifying colour and can turn the look of an expensive hotel.

Yellow is another declassifier. It signals cheapness, temporariness and caution. Yellow is the colour that the eyes register the quickest and the one likeliest to stop traffic or sell a house. Even a single row of yellow marigolds growing outside a home for sale will hasten the payment of the booking deposit for it. Since yellow also signals caution, it is preferred for rental cars, school buses and taxis, but not for banks. Splashes of yellow such as in a bouquet of flowers are cheering but excess of it tends to increase anxiety and cause tempers to flare. Babies cry more frequently and with greater gusto in the presence of yellow. Temperamental artists, opera singers, writers and musicians are also seem to explode the quickest in yellow rooms.

Forest green and burgundy are classifying colours. These two shades are preferred by the wealthiest persons. Colours that classify elevate certain product's position or target some specific buying population. Red is being marketed in a blue based red container and is selling with a great success. Women inherit a preference for bluish red while men seem to favour yellowish red.

Red, a classifier, has many virtues. It makes people unaware of how much time is passing and is therefore the colour of choice of casinos and bars. Studies show that red makes food more aromatic and entices people into eating more. Even if you shun the red cherries because of their red dye they seem to make a better tasting fruit salad.

These are few examples by which we can nearly establish the pull due to colour. The pull intensity depends on the type of colour and it can be used to enchance the appeal of things and places.

4

Healing with Colours

The medicines and their studies have been the part and parcel of the history of man's health and diseases since the dawn of civilization. The goals of medicines have always been to promote good health, prevent disease, restore health and rehabilitate the patient. Healing with colour helps achieve all these goals.

Colours or colour-radiated medicines have been administered as a therapeutic means down the ages. In this chapter we will learn about many methods of healing the human diseases with colours, and various latest applications being tested in research programmes.

Colours have been adopted as a cure to illness. Specific ailments can be cured by adjusting the required colour input to the body. Colour therapy, in fact, is becoming an accepted and established part of clinical and medical office setting. The power of colour healing has been recognised by most health professionals around the world who practise advanced medical techniques, especially those utilising method of non-traditional and complementary medicines, such as visualisation and imagery orthomolecular nutrition, acupuncture/acupressure, Reiki, biofeed back and electromagnetics.

Radionic Research Using Colour Therapy

It has been established that very deep red and blue colours speed up and slow down, respectively, the metabolism and overall growth of plants. These colours similarly affect human beings. For instance, red light has been found to speed up the circulation and raise blood pressure, while blue light is calming. The effect is found same even if the patient is blind or blindfolded.

The theory of radionic is that every part of the human body radiates a specific level of energy. If all these energies are at specific levels, the individual etheric body is in balance. The etheric body is the spiritual essence of the physical body, but it exists in abstract form and is thus non-tangible. It carries the spark of life and can be reviewed externally as the colour of the Aura. If an individual's energy levels are either too high or too low, the etheric body is out of balance or in disharmony. Disharmony in etheric body can result in disease in the physical body. According to the radionic theory, nothing occurs in the physical body unless it first happens in the etheric body.

The colour therapy when applied to an individual's multicoloured Aura, brings about a harmony for the person. People with psychic healing abilities can be trained to see the multicoloured Aura, which is said to be an electromagnetic field, extending out about three feet around the entire body. A few say they can even diagnose diseases by interpreting the intensity of each colour and the distance each colour extends out from the body.

In fact, colour can affect people's mood, perception of temperature and time and their ability to concentrate. The colour therapy is now being increasingly used to produce desired responses in mental health clinics, hospital recovery rooms, prison cells and in workplaces.

Radionic Healing in Action

Each colour of light vibrates at a different frequency. The colour vibrations reach the patient's etheric body and energise it to start vibrating and do what it should be doing. Before treating a patient with the radionics for any particular illness, the colour therapist must first clean out the person's Aura. *This is necessary* because Aura may contain ruptures or leaks. Ruptures can occur in the patient's body during application of anesthesia in the event of an accident, due to emotional shock or high fever, and so on.

5

The Basic Postulates of Colour Healing

Before we discuss the basic postulation of colour healing, here are two important points to remember:
a) The different colours can be used to achieve certain responses.

Physical responses to colours are neither tied to our individual psyches nor do they bear much relation to our cultural background. In fact, everyone has the same physical responses to certain colours.

b) Even colour-blind individuals, who can't identify the colours, react to colours in the same way as the normal people.

All earthy objects such as plants, animals, human beings and other living things have their own characteristic frequency of vibration.

All living cells, tissues, organs and other human body parts have their own characteristic frequency of vibration in health.

Illness is an altered physiological functioning that is the body's natural response to stress. Altered functioning is nothing more than a change in frequency with the stepping up or lowering of the vibration caused by a stressor. The stressor can be generated from a chemical, mechanical (physical) or thermal source. Mental and emotional stressors help to change a frequency when they cause an internal chemical response, such as hormonal stimulation.

- All illnesses have a characteristic frequency of vibration.

- Applying a corrective frequency in the form of food, physical therapy, injection, nutrients, oral drugs, exercise, colour or some other methods of healing, will help the distressed body function return to its homeostatic pattern.
- Body cells selectively take in normal rays and vibration from the environment when they need them. However, if the environment presents overly strong rays and vibrations, the cells will absorb them even when they don't need or want them.
- Cells that lack colour vibrations, just like as cells that lack nutrition, will tend to de-polarise and alter their frequencies and therefore their pattern of growth. If too much colour is present in the immediate environment of cells, it will overcharge them to such a degree that their frequencies and growth pattern will alter to the point of damage.
- Like a toxic food, a wrong colour can change the electromagnetic force field or frequency of a cell, which sets up a chain reaction. The change of frequency will interact with a larger field of force of the organ which in turn will affect the body system. This will have an adverse effect upon the individual. Such a chain of reactions can lead to chronic fatigue syndrome.
- The fatigue may then bring exhaustion in the organisms and eventually lead to death.
- Colour as pure vibration is the rational therapy for maintaining health and overcoming disease (as a complementary or alternative treatment to traditional allopathic medicines or drug treatments) because it presents itself for the body's use in the right form (or food) at the right place and at the right time.
- Colour can readily be adopted for clinical application by physicians who practise orthomolecular medicine.
- In some specific cases, therapists prefer to direct the colours at specific parts of the body instead of bathing the whole body in colour.
- The most vital advantage is that application of colour therapy is not at all regarded as harmful to the body and mind.

Ultraviolet Radiation Therapy

In an unpublished manuscript on photopherisis (the medical potential of ultraviolet light) regarding physiologic actions and effects of ultraviolet energy, it is mentioned that when UV ray's photoluminescense is absorbed by the bloodstream, the first effect is physical, then chemical and finally biological. Photochemical reactions are initiated by change of electronic configuration and velocity. If the incident energy is short enough, it will produce vibrations in the electrons which will then be activated. These electrons may then be ejected and the molecule is thus ionised or they may be displaced to an outer orbit and then the atom or molecule is activated. Photoelectric phenomena are the basis of all the subsequent reactions.

The following reactions take place in the human body when the ultraviolet energy strikes it.

- Calcium metabolism is profoundly improved by an increased blood content.
- Bacteria in the body are killed by the direct action of the UV rays and indirectly by increased local and systemic resistance.
- Toxins in the body are rendered inert.
- Normal chemical balances in the body are restored.
- Cellular imbalance in the blood is corrected if UV is administered in suitable doses.
- Oxygen absorption is increased following UV irradiation of autotransfused blood.

- The immune system is depressed, the immune resistance to bacterial infection is lessened and the bactericidal potency of the blood is reduced with a fall in haemoglobin by an overdosage of UV.

Individuals vary greatly in their sensitiveness to ultraviolet irradiation regarding systemic and skin effects. Sensitivity to it is cumulative.

The action of ultraviolet rays may be immediate, somewhat delayed, markedly delayed or protracted on any individual. Ultraviolet irradiation acutely illustrates the power of colour on all people.

Healing Colours for Certain Dysfunctions

Now question arises as to which spectral colours are useful in the treatment of pathological conditions besides the unseen colour of UV?

Colours are most readily applied to a specific dysfunctional human or animal body parts or organs in the form of coloured lights. Various shades of each colour are employed by therapists depending on the strength of their physiological effect.

Red

Red stimulates the sensory nerves, so it benefits the senses of smell, sight, hearing, taste and touch. It activates blood circulation, excites the cerebrospinal fluid and rouses the sympathetic nervous system. Haemoglobin is built with red rays. Red rays produce heat that vitalises and energises the liver, the muscular system and the left cerebral brain hemisphere. As a muscle relaxant, red counters spasm, its irritant effects are excellent for therapeutic purposes.

Red decomposes the body's accumulated salt crystals and thus catalyses ionisation. The ions created then carry electromagnetic energy throughout the body. The rays split ferric-salt crystals and liberate heat.

Common Disorders treatable with Red Colour include:
Anaemia
Listlessness
Asthma
Paralysis
Blood Dyscrasias
Physical Debilitation
Bronchitis
Pneumonia
Constipation
Tuberculosis
Endocrine System Dysfunction

Conditions contraindicated for using Red Colour include:
Emotional disturbances
Hypertension
Excitable temperament
Mental illness
Fever
Neuritis
Florid complexion
Red hair
Inflammations

Yellow

Yellow activates the motor nerves and generates the energy for the muscles. A disturbance in the supply of yellow vibrations to any part of the body can bring about a disturbance of function there including partial or full paralysis. Yellow, as a mixture of red and green rays, has the stimulating potency of red vibrations mixed with the reparative potency of green vibrations. Therefore, it tends both to stimulate function and repair damages.

Directed at the gastrointestinal tract for short periods, yellow is a digestive aid. For longer periods, it acts as both a catharsis (Purge) and a cathartic (Laxative). It helps to eliminate parasites and worms and stimulates the flow of bile.

Nerve building takes place in the presence of yellow. It has a stimulating, cleansing and eliminating action on the liver, intestines and skin. It energises the alimentary tract, purifies the blood stream, activates the lymphatics and depresses the spleen. It lifts despondency and brings joy, gaiety, intellect perception and merriment.

Common Disorders treatable with Yellow Colour include:
Arthritis and rheumatism
Digestive problems
Constipation
Eczema
Diabetes
Exhaustion
Flatulence
Liver disease
Hemiplegia
Mental depression
Indigestion
Paralysis
Kidney disease
Paraplegia

Conditions contraindicated for using Yellow Colour include:
Acute inflammation
Heart palpitation
Delirium
Neuralgia
Diarrhoea
Overexcitement
Fever

Orange

Orange combines red and yellow rays and its heating power is greater than that of either red or yellow alone. Orange stimulates the thyroid glands and depresses the parathyroid. It expands the lungs and has an antispasmodic effect on muscle cramps. It also aids calcium metabolism, acts as an emetic and increases the pulse rate, but orange does not affect the blood pressure. Milk production in the breast is stimulated after child birth when the mother wears orange clothing. Orange also acts on the spleen and pancreas to help assimilation and circulation.

Common Disorders treatable with Orange Colour include:

Asthma
Kidney ailments
Bronchitis
Menstrual difficulties
Cold
Mental exhaustion
Epilepsy
Prolapsed uterus
Gallstones
Respiratory diseases
Gout
Rheumatism and arthritis
Hyperthyroidism
Tumors (both malignant and benign)
Hypothyroidism

Note: Conditions contraindicated for using the orange colour are not known.

Green

Green, both dark and pastel shades, builds muscles, bones and other tissue cells. It is neither acidic nor alkaline and can be used the same way as blue is used. Green is soothing, cooling and calming, both physically and mentally. It relieves tension, lowers blood pressure, acts as a hypnotic upon the sympathetic nervous system, dilates the capillaries and produces a sense of warmth.

Green rays help to stabilise the emotions and stimulate the pituitary. They can be used for their aphrodisiac quality and for sexual tonicity. Vibrations of green disinfect bacteria, virus and other germs.

Common Disorders treatable with Green Colour include:
Asthma
Laryngitis
Malaria
Back problems
Colic
Malignancy
Erysipelas
Nervous disorder
Exhaustion
Neuralgia
Hay fever
Overstimulation
Heart problems
Syphilis
Haemorrhoids
Typhoid fever
Insomnia
Ulcer
Irritability
Venereal disease

Note: Conditions contraindicated for using the green colour are not known.

Blue

Blue vibratory rays increase the metabolism, build vitality, promote growth, slow down the action of heart and act as a tonic on the body in general. They have antiseptic properties, contracting potency for muscles and blood vessels and a soothing or cooling effect on inflammations.

Blue is the balancing and harmonising colour that regulates the blood stream to normal. It reduces the nervous excitement. It is an astringent and can be absorbed from the environment during meditation and spiritual expansion. It relaxes the mind. It helps the introvert come out of his shell and comfort the maniac-depressiveness. But after ten minutes of concentrated treatments with blue rays, mental depression tends to set in. However, blue clothings and furnishings sometimes make a person tired.

Blue is the colour of truth, devotion, calmness, sincerity, intuition with higher mental faculties.

Common Disorders treatable with Blue Colour include:

Baldness
Biliousness
Bowel irregularity
Burns
Cataracts
Chicken pox
Cholera
Colic
Constipation
Diarrhoea
Dysentery
Epilepsy
Eye inflammation
Febrile diseases
Glaucoma
Goitre
Gonorrhoea
Headache
Heart palpitations
Hydrophobia
Hysteria
Insomnia
Itching
Jaundice
Laryngitis

Measles
Menstrual difficulties
Poliomyelitis
Renal (Kidney) diseases
Rheumatism (acute)
Scarlet fever
Shock
Skin diseases
Syphilis
Tonsillitis
Tooth infection
Typhoid fever
Ulcer
Vomiting
Whooping cough

Conditions contraindicated for using Blue Colour include:
Cold
Gout
Hypertension
Muscle impairment
Paralysis
Rheumatism (chronic)
Tachycardia

Indigo

Indigo is a soothing and cooling astringent. It is a parathyroid stimulant and thyroid depressant, and a blood purifier. It reduces or stops excessive bleeding and promotes muscular tonicity, respiratory depression and hypnotic-like insensibility to pain.

Indigo rays control the psychic currents of the subtle spiritual bodies. They also control the forehead chakra and influence vision, hearing and smell on the physical, emotional and spiritual planes.

Known Disorders treatable with Indigo Colour include:
Appendicitis
Asthma
Bronchitis
Cataract
Convulsion
Deafness
Deurium tremens
Dyspepsia
Ear diseases
Eye diseases ❋
Hyperthyroidism
Mental illness
Nasal diseases
Nervous ailments
Nose bleeding
Obsession
Palsy
Pneumonia
Respiratory diseases
Throat diseases

Note: Conditions contraindicated for using the indigo colour are not known.

Violet

Violet stimulates the spleen, upper brain and bones. It depresses the lymphatics, heart muscles and motor nerves. Violet is calming in cases of mental illness. It controls irritability, reduces hunger, builds leucocytes and maintains ionic balance especially of potassium and sodium. *The power of meditation can be ten times greater under violet light falling through the stained glass window.*

Known Disorders treatable with Violet Colour include:
Bladder problem
Bone growth dysfunction

Cerebrospinal meningitis
Concussion
Cramps (abdominal)
Kidney disease
Mental illness
Nervous disorders
Neuralgia
Rheumatism (acute & chronic)
Scalp diseases
Sciatica
Skin diseases
Tumors (benign and malignant)

Note: Conditions contraindicated for using the violet colour are not known.

Ultraviolet

Ultraviolet has chemical and bacteriocidal properties that break down bacterial toxins. Ultraviolet light at the extreme end of the colour spectrum accelerates the lymphatic and circulatory system, antibody production, grandular activity and metabolism. It also enhances the action of the lungs, heart and sympathetic nervous system.

Known Disorders treatable with Ultraviolet Colour include:
Goitre
Gonorrhoea
Heart disease
Respiratory disease
Rickets
Syphilis
Ulcers
Wounds

Conditions contraindicated for using the ultraviolet colour include malignant melanoma and other skin cancers.

The diseases and conditions listed above as being healed or affected by specific colours are only a sampling. They are the disorders that have been verified as being highly responsive to colour treatment. Advanced techniques now offer new avenues of promoting well-being for the patients who are benefited immensely.

7

Advanced Colour Therapy

Sunlight includes a broad spectrum of rays. The ones that tan are the ultraviolet rays (UVs) and they pass directly through the outer layer of the skin to affect the more sensitive lower layers. There is scientific confirmation that the UV rays travel beyond the skin into other parts of the body to produce either a healing or destructive effect depending on which form of UV is predominant.

In fact, the sun rays also emit wavelengths not visible to human eye—for example, infrared rays, ultraviolet rays, and X-rays. Although the eye is not sensitive to these invisible rays, the body is, and it may be helped or harmed by them.

Ultraviolet B (UVB) rays are shorter and are the primary cause of sunburns. Ninety per cent of their effect is on the skin surface and only ten per cent on underneath. The tan a person gets on his skin surface from UVB rays helps him to protect his underneath skin surface from sunburns. Ultraviolet A (UVA) rays are longer. They do 90 per cent of their damage on the supporting inner layers of the skin and have at least ten times the wrinkling-effect as UVBs. The tan obtained from UVA rays does not protect against sunburns (as often erroneously claimed by tanning salons). However, UVA and UVB rays have both negative and positive photo-chemotherapeutic effects on human physiology and pathology.

The Principles of Advanced Colour Therapy

According to modern colour therapists, there are seventeen principles of colour healing. None of these principles calls for the use of chemicals alone, which is done ordinarily in the allopathic prescription of chemotherapy.

The application of colour for ushering good health, emotional stability and spiritual elevation is made most effective by following these seventeen principles.

1. Colour can be introduced into a person through various methods, such as coloured foods, solarised (exposed to sun) liquids and solids. Sunlight or artificial rays are also applied to the skin. Contrasting coloured room decor, coloured clothing, birthstones, crystals and gems can also be used in colour therapy. Meditation on and in colour, coloured lights and colour breathing change the consciousness of an individual and help him reach his Aura or electromagnetic force field.

2. In colour therapy, either the colour that the diseased person lacks, is supplied or the overabundant colour that is unbalancing the body, is reduced. The overabundant colour is also neutralised by furnishing its complementary shade.

3. The two foundation colours of colour healing are *red* and *blue*. All other colours are subsidiaries or refinements of red and blue.

4. The required coloured lights should be applied at the most strategic time and in the most suitable manner to the human body systems, organs, parts, tissues and cell structures.

5. The pure the colour, the more penetrating the rays and the faster the body's reaction.

6. When in doubt, undertreat the patient, rather than giving him too much colour treatment.

7. Don't overload one system of the body to help its other system. Be careful not to load the circulatory system with the eliminating toxins produced by invading micro-organisms when treating an infection.

8. Overexposure to one colour can be remedied by applying the complementary colour.
9. If the wrong colour is accidentally used, first neutralise the wrong colour with its complementary colour, then treat the disease condition with the correct colour.
10. When planning for colour therapy either for yourself or someone else, take into account the circumstances under which the treatment will be delivered. For instance, you may need to apply the colour as white light behind a colour filter. Other circumstances to be considered could be the colour medium, any sensitivity of the patient, the quality of the colour filter, the nature of the disease, the extent of pathology, the weather and climate, the required colour, the time of the day, the season of the year and the patient's biorhythm. (The biorhythm is a biologically inherent cyclic variation or recurrence of an event or state such as the sleep cycle, circadian rhythms and periodic diseases.)
11. Natural colour is more powerful healer than the colour in glass, filters and dyes. It is the power to transmit colour rather than the visual effect of colour that is important in healing.
12. Misapplied colour can deteriorate certain body parts. For instance, misused bright red colour shocks the eyes and leads to fatigue and irritation in general. A red room raises the blood pressure, a green one lowers it.
13. Colour rays absorbed through the skin affect all the glands, blood cells and chemicals in the body.
14. Colour in clothings and hair dyes affect the entire body.
15. Both artificial lights (such as from incandescent bulb) and that of natural light from the sun rays heal by the process of oxidation and metabolic enhancement.
16. Healing with colour aims to re-establish body balance and release tension caused by colour starvation.
17. To treat a specific organ first select its appropriate trigger points and then apply appropriate colours on them.

In colour therapy, a main colour and complementary colours are used. The complementary pairings are red and turquoise, orange and blue, yellow and violet, green and magenta.

Note: In modern techniques, the therapist compiles a detailed spine chart and uses it to explain to the patient which colours will be used for therapy and why. Generally, seven or more weekly treatment sessions are required. Colour therapy instruments are also used now. For instance, a colour therapy instrument beams coloured lights on the patient through shaped apertures.

Colour Breathing

To alter the imbalanced electromagnetic forces to bring them in harmony, the technique most effectively employed is to meditate while performing colour breathing. In the technique of colour breathing, developed by yoga teachers, the one concentrates on the desired colour mentally, using it in one's respiration process and meditates.

The best time to practise colour breathing is immediately following or preceding breakfast or dinner (not lunch). Colour breathing should not be practised as the last exercise of the night during the first month of employing the technique, because it is too stimulating to the mind and spirit. The increase of vital force may prevent sleep. The controlled colour breathing not only raises the body vibrations but it also unites you subjectively with universal consciousness. You should try to be fully aware during the exercise of the inflow of colour rays revitalising your body and mind systems and replenishing the finer vehicles of personal healing power with cosmic energy.

Procedure for Colour Healing

Breathe rhythmically from twelve to eighteen times a minute. You may frame your timings prior to meditation to establish the inhalation-exhalation pattern. As you respirate in this steady rhythm, you should visualise the colours of the spectrum. If you are attempting to overcome a certain condition, you should use one particular colour or its nearest equivalent as your healing agent. Here are the step-by-step techniques for correct colour breathing:

First: Imagine yourself engulfed by a white light from the cosmos that enters your body through your head and moves down to your extremities. See it flood your entire being from within and outside. Hold on to this image for at least two minutes.

Second: Draw from this spectrum of white light the colour specifically required for the healing process you desire to achieve.

Third: Visualise red, yellow and orange being drawn up from the earth through the soles of your feet to your various organs. This is the force known as *Kundalini* as explained in our old shastras.

In contrast, visualise blue, violet and indigo as arriving from atmosphere. You will visualise these colours as vertical rays entering your body through the anterior, frontal and penetrating into the various organs. In our shastras, the atmospheric force is known as *Prana*.

Also, visualise green coming into your body through your navel on the horizontal plane.

Fourth: After employing the necessary colour mentally, bathe your body in white light, allowing yourself fully to be engulfed in it. White light begins and ends the self-treatment with colour breathing.

The colour healer is a deep breather who is conscious of the universal life-spirit that is around him. The universal life-spirit lends healing strength. With each deep breathing, the colour healer draws himself a portion of this power. He does this inhalation while consciously feeling the grandeur of being in harmony with the infinite.

Treatment Trigger Points For Organs and Body Parts

The trigger point in an Aura of the body is that point which on bombarding with colour affects its related body system organs, tissues or other parts dramatically and drastically. Some of the vital areas that act as trigger points include the body's six nerve centres, the seven major chakras and some subsidiary chakras plus the frontals of the head, the carotid arteries and the gluteal muscle area.

Certain areas of the body are more important than others when they are treated with colour. *The most important treatment points are the nerve centres in the spine and the solar plexus. These are* followed in importance by the forehead, the back of neck, the chest and the abdomen. In general, treatment should be administered to strengthen the human body as a whole. Sometimes, however, local applications are also employed.

The chakras are bell-shaped vortices (whirling, eddying areas of power). In the etheric (non-physical) body, each chakra has a characteristic colour and intersects with the spinal cord at a definite point. They are specialised channels of colour force. The individual colour of each chakra relates directly to the healing colour for the specific body area near to which the chakra is located.

The size and configuration of the chakras depend on the individual person and his stage of development in the astral, mental and spiritual aspects of life. Each chakra absorbs a special current of vital energy through its particular colour ray from the physical environment and from the higher levels of consciousness.

Just as we have seven major chakras and seven endocrine systems (glands) for secreting the hormones, so do we have seven vital force centres which are linked with the operation of seven *brains*. (The seven bodies are labelled as *organic, nervous, etheric, astral, mental, casual* and *buddic* that interpenetrate each other because of their discriminating subtle etheric and atomic structure). Each chakra is spinning at a different rate of vibration called frequency. The study of these frequencies continuing from ancient India to the present day. The word chakra means "wheel" and is an ancient Indian symbol, used in this sense to mean a centre of physical and psychic energy.

By controlling the frequency of these chakras, we control their positive or negative spinning. It gives us conscious control over the positive and negative functions of the brain and helps us control our own destiny. Instead of pumping all our consciousness into electronic computers and complex engineering systems, our next evolutionary step is to learn to become engineer of our own consciousness and of the forces in society which are reflections of our inner world. If even a small group of people come together and practise the awakening of the total number of cells in the human brain, the energies which will develop, could liberate the enormous potential of mankind for a new age.

Trigger Points and Their Treatment

Treatment with appropriate colour should be administered at specific trigger points of the human body to achieve the desired healing effect. The following is a listing of correct therapeutic colours to apply to particular organs and body systems.

The Brain

Use *indigo, blue* or *violet* colour to quiet the blood and the nerves of the scalp, face, back, neck and feet in order to calm the brain.

To do this, *shine the light in these areas*, expose the vision for brief moments to the appropriate coloured light so that it can reach the brain also through eyes.

The Heart

Use *violet, indigo* and *blue* for soothing purposes, apply colour therapy to the chest, primarily over the heart, and then feet and arms to stimulate the blood and nerves. Apply orange colour over these areas.

Cerebro-Spinal System

Use *yellow* and *violet*, treat right side of the head.

Circulatory System

Use *dark green* for its calming effect, treat the whole body. To invigorate, use *grass green,* use *bright red* if there is no elevated blood pressure, *blue* can be substituted for *green.*

Upper & Lower Extremities

Use *red* colour to correct the impairment of the muscle structures, excepting the situation when shock is involved.

Endocrine System

At the site of endocrine glands, use *green* to comfort all the endocrine glands and then *blue* to activate them.

Abdomen & Loins
Use *red, orange* and *yellow* to stimulate the gastric juices, blood nerves and peristaltic action of the gastrointestinal tract. Apply the colour to the lower back, groin hips, feet and abdominal area, especially the navel region. To overcome diarrhoea and inflammation, apply *blue*, *violet* and *indigo*. Treat the epigastrium with *blue* for psychological disturbances. For trouble in the loins, such as hernia or intestinal rapture, use the *red* spectrum. Treat with *green* for its tonic effect on general abdominal region. Treat with *yellow* to stimulate the epigastric nerves, and use *blue* to relax the abdominal muscles when they are cramped.

Kidney and Urinary System
Apply *yellow* to lower back, groin, loin, hips and feet.

Lungs and Respiratory System
Use *yellow* and *violet* on the middle of the sternum on a line with the second rib.

Musculo-Skeletal System
Apply *red* rays to the left side of the head.

The Neck and Thorax
Treat them with *purple*.

The Nervous System
Use *violet* and *lavender* to soothe the right and left sides of the brain. Apply grass green for its invigorative effect, and medium *yellow* and *orange* for their stimulating effect.

The Skin
Treat local patches of skin with yellow.

Sex Organs
Use colour indicated for local area, such as *yellow* for ovaries, uterus, testes and prostrate because they are situated near the kidneys and urinary systems.

The Rectum
Treat it as listed for kidneys with the colour determined by the specific condition.

Sunspots Effect
It has now been proven that colour-ray frequency changes arising out of sunspots effect, the flocculation index of human blood. Flocculation is a biological reaction in which normally invisible material leaves a liquid solution to form a course suspension or precipitate as a result of a change in physical or chemical conditions. During this biological reaction, the liquid solution may change its colour and become easily recognisable.

Flocculation tests using blood serum and special reagents (solutions) are useful in diagnosing liver abnormalities and other aspects of normal and abnormal human physiology (pathology).

Uses and Benefits of Sun Rays
Whatever is in existence in this universe has specific colour for recognition. On the other hand, different colours of sun rays and their elements are being used in preparation of medicines all over the world. In sun rays therapy, these colours are used directly in preparation of medicines. These medicines, produced at a very low cost, are within the reach of the common people.

The seven main colours of sun rays are:
1. Violet
2. Indigo
3. Blue
4. Green
5. Yellow
6. Orange
7. Red

Thanks to their healing properties, the rays of these colours can replace a vast quantity of allopathic medicines used for various diseases.

Properties Regarding Temperament (Basic Nature) of Coloured Rays

First, it is very important for a healer to know the basic temperament of colour which he is using on the patient for his cure. The healer should use only the desired colour as per requirement of the body to cure a particular disease.

1. *Violet, Blue, Indigo*: They have cool and soothing temperament.
2. *Yellow, Orange, Red*: They have the warm and stimulating temperament.
3. *Green:* It is the only colour, which has got normal/medium effect. It is *blood purifier* and *harmonizer*.

Methods For Application of Sun Rays Therapy

1. **By Using Coloured Radiation on the Body:** The patient is being exposed to sun in between the required colour sheets. Patient is allowed to lay down in appropriate position with exposure of body parts where the required coloured light is to be emitted through the coloured glass positioning in between sun and the patient.
2. **Preparation of Medicines by Absorption of Coloured Rays in Materials:** Eatables and liquids are kept in desired coloured transparent pots with tight caps exposed to the direct sun rays in any open space for specific period till the material in pots absorbs the desired degree of potency of the coloured radiations from the sun. However, detailed procedure after exposure to sun light for using the medicine will be explained in the following chapters.

Type of Materials which can be Radiated

a) These may include water, sugar, milk, honey, glycerine, rose water and oils etc.
b) Oils are prepared and solarized to make medicines for body massage and local applications.

c) Empty bottles charged in the sun are used for colour breathing in many cases.

Methods for Preparation of Medicines

Water: Sun rays can be used to immense benefits by getting them absorbed (radiated) in our eatables and drinking materials, in required/desired coloured form. Generally, water is used to prepare the cheapest radiated medicines which are easily available. Bottles of suitable/desired colour are hygienically washed and cleaned and fresh water is filled and sealed. Precaution must be taken to fill the bottles below the neck for free movement of the filled liquids, or by filling them only 3-4th of their capacity. After filling and sealing, the bottles are kept in any open space exposed to sun light at least eight hours a day. The coloured radiations will be absorbed by the bottle contents in conformity with the colour of the bottle. Precautions should be taken daily for regular dust cleaning and sterilization of the material filled in, so that maximum sun rays can be absorbed by the material kept in the bottle for its proper medication. Generally when enough radiations for exposure are available, medicine is ready for use in emergency cases within eight hours. However, it should be kept aside for minimum period of three days before its use for getting better results from the medicine thus prepared.

Precaution should also be observed while exposing the bottles to sunlight. Their shadow should not overlap each other. Bottles should be kept in such a way that distance in between them be equal to their heights. The different coloured bottles should not be kept at the same place because chances of mixing of their properties and potential values are there. Only similar coloured bottles should be kept together at one place. *This is very important from medical point of view for keeping the medicinal potentiality intact.*

It has also been observed that if *green* or *blue* bottles are kept exposed to sun light after filling the liquid material continuously for 7 to 8 days, their applications get maximum results. It has very positive medicinal effect on high blood pressure, infections and urinal problem of the patients.

Sugar and Misri: While sending the medicines to distant places, it is found very difficult to transport the liquid glass containers.

Chances of their breakage are very high. In such cases we can send sugar, misri or sugar milk, prepared by coloured radiations in the same way (i.e. by keeping in coloured glass pots and exposed to direct sun light for at least 8 hours a day for 45 days or more) for the use of patient in prescribed dosages depending upon its medicinal values.

Oils: Generally oils are used for body massages or external applications. Oils are prepared through the same process of radiation effect in desired colour, keeping in view the required medicinal value.

Blue Oil: As per requirement, the blue radiations are applied to the patient to provide maximum cooling effect in the process of treatment. Mustard and coconut oils are most suitable for the purpose.

Red Oil: Red radiations are provided to the patient for the healing effect needed for remedy of pains. Red oil is prepared from Til seeds. For its preparation, red coloured bottles are cleaned and filled up with Til oil and kept exposed to sun to absorb maximum radiations at least eight hours a day for 45 days continuously. If bottles are kept for longer span, it gives more and better results.

Glycerine: It should be kept in cleaned blue coloured bottles in open space to be charged by sun light for at least 45 days. If it is kept for more days, it will be more effective. It can be used in emergency cases after 7 days. It is very good for treatment of swollen and infected *tonsils, gums, toothache, soar throat and rashes on the skin. It can also be used on face for soothing the facial skin and muscles.*

Miracles of Green Radiated Water

Prepare the green water as described in the method of preparation of water medicines. After at least seven days of complete radiation (absorbing of green rays), water can be used for eye diseases like:

Sore eyes

Granules or irritation

Eye's watering

Pollution or dust effect

Eye's redness
Weak eyesight
And first stage of cataract

You have to wash your eyes with green water only twice/thrice a day to get the miraculous effect in shortest possible time.

Note: Bottles are to be kept in open where maximum sun rays are available for longer period. Many feel that moon light has the adverse effect. It deteriorates the sun rays effect. *In fact,* there is no adverse effect of moon light on sun radiated medicines. All bottles should be cleaned of dust daily for proper sun radiations on medicines.

- For blue coloured bottles, empty and cleaned bottles of milk of magnesia or vicks can be used.
- For orange bottles, empty beer or scotch brown bottles can be used after cleaning.
- For green bottles, scotch and beer bottles can be used after cleaning.

Dosages of the Prepared Medicines

Medicines for Drinking

An average dosage of 1 to 3 oz (i.e. 7 ml to 20 ml) is prescribed if fully charged or 25–35 ml if less charged. Taking medicine thrice or four times a day is sufficient for the patient suffering from general ailments. In emergency or acute/chronic diseases, number of dosages can be increased depending upon requirement.

- In cases of children, dosages are to be given according to their age (i.e. taking into consideration the quantity of dosage and span of times). Children under twelve years of age are generally given half dose.
- In case of overdosage, immediately white or green energised water has to be consumed for balancing the adverse effects to the extent of minimum reaction.
- Energised sugar/misri dosage for adults is 1 gram.
- Green energised water can be taken up to 1 cup.

- In chronic diseases, medicine is to be given twice/four times a day as per requirement.
- In emergency cases, frequent dosages can be recommended.

Causes of Illness

The naturo-therapist as well as the patients must know that except *epidemics,* all other diseases are caused by accumulation of *morbid* and *toxic* matter in the body. These morbid and toxic materials are accumulated in the body by wrong eating habits. Though different diseases have different names but the root cause lies in the wrong eating habits.

Acute Diseases: When the body is full of toxic and morbid matters, it tries to convert these into adverse matters in the form of *fever, urine infection, cold* and other such diseases. These are known as acute diseases in the common language.

Chronic Diseases: If during the course of treatment, disease is suppressed by intake of strong medicine then the toxic matter remains in the body and infects one or other part of the body. In such a case, multi-problem diseases generate inside the body which then turn into chronic diseases as we often term them. Their treatment is long, sometimes it continues throughout the life. Therefore, before prescribing any dosage of medicine to the patient, care may be taken to assess the temperament of patient's body.

To assess the temperament of any patient's body, a simple questionnaire should be formulated. You can assess the temperament and cause of disease by examining the replies of the patient to your questionnaire. Accordingly you may decide the course of your proposed treatment.

For detailed analysis of the disease, the following methods be checked out carefully by asking and observing the patient, so that you can properly diagnose the disease.

Diagnosis of Patient on the Basis of His/Her Physical Symptoms

S. No.	Diagnosis	Symptoms		
		Heat	Cough	Wind (Impurity of Blood)
1.	Tongue colour	Red	White	Dirty
2.	Mouth taste	Bitter	Tasteless	Bad
3.	Thirst	Extra/Over-thirst	Less/Under-thirst	–
4.	Appetite	–	Less	–
5.	Abdomen bowels	Hard	Soft	Constipation
6.	Quantity of urine	Less	Frequent	Less
7.	Colour of urine	Dark yellow	White	Dirty
8.	Colour of eyes	Redness	White	Dirtiness
9.	Physical body	Slim	Fatty	–
10.	Physical body references	Hot	Cold	Dry
11.	Perspiration	Extra	Less	Very little
12.	Age	Weight	Height	

Asking the patient about the following habits:

13. Eating Habits
    – Vegetarian
    – Non-Vegetarian
    – Hard drinks habit

    Atta – with husk/without husk
    Rice – coarse/refined

14. Smoking/Chewing
    – Pan masala
    – Tobacco
    – Cigarette
    – Bidi

15. Drinking
    – Tea
    – Coffee
    – Soft drinks
      Number of times

| 16. | Colour affinity | Which colour he/she likes normally. (It is a general tendency of the patient to like the colour which is less in the body). |

The above information in the chart will help in diagnosing the disease to a great extent.

Treatment of Diseases

After physical diagnosis and understanding the disease of the patient, treatment should be taken up.

1. **Bile Disease:** When toxic materials inside our body are being deposited more than extreme limit, body heat increases. Due to extra heat in the body the *bile* disease occurs.

   As we know, *Blue* colour has the maximum *cooling effect*, so it is always advised to have *Blue Medicine*. Here I mean the blue radiated medicine. Blue radiation may however be applied directly to the body parts affected by the disease.

2. **Cough Disease:** When the body temperature is being disturbed due to one or other reasons, it becomes much lower than the normal. The low body temperature leads to the development of cough in the body.

   In such cases, hot radiations are very useful and these are obtained from red radiations. Therefore, *Red Medicine* and *Red Radiations* are very much helpful in this disease condition.

3. **Wind Disease:** The root cause of such type of diseases is excess accumulation of morbid and toxic materials in the body, thus developing impurity in the blood. Impurity in blood causes wind diseases. For treating such type of diseases *Green Medicines* and *Green Radiations* are very effective.

At a Glance

Bile Disease : Body generates excess heat.
Blue medicine and Blue radiations to be given.

Cough Disease : It is because of low body temperature.
Red medicine and Red radiations to be given.

Wind Disease : The root cause is accumulation of morbid and toxic matters. Means impurity of blood. Green medicine & Green radiations to be given.

According to the science of colour therapy, the human body needs different colours for different organs of body as per their need to cure their malfunctioning, as described below:

Head & Neck portions	: Blue
Throat	: Dark blue
Chest & Lungs	: Violet
Intestines & Kidney	: Green
Rectum and surroundings	: Green
Skin	: Green
Liver	: Yellow
Dysentery	: Orange
Cold and painful body	: Red

Radiation

If radiation of the required colour is directly given to malfunctioning parts of the body and surrounding areas for nearly 1 to 2 hrs continuously, miraculous results are seen after treatment for at least 15 continuous days. This coloured radiation has its own pure natural effects on the body without any side effects. If problem is related to a particular organ or part of the body, application of same coloured radiated oil and its massage on that part along with direct colour therapy will enhance the pace of recovery from disease.

Swelling and Redness (Skin Allergy) of body can be relieved by application of *Blue oil* and *Blue radiations* in natural ways without any side effect within a short period. On the other hand if the disease is old and chronic, application of red radiated oil with red radiations will relieve the swelling and redness of skin in the shortest period.

Similarly in the case of high fevers, *iced blue piece of cloth (patti) in blue radiated water with blue radiations will give you miraculous results without any side effect.*

If you are a *chronic asthmatic patient, use orange coloured empty bottles with cork or cap (charged in air only) three to four times for immediate relief.*

Properties of Prime Colours

Basically, three main colours, *Blue, Green & Red* dominate our body and we are dependant on these primary colours. These colours are being used for preparation of radiated water and direct application of colour radiations.

Certain properties of these prime colours are described below for the benefit of the common people who are really interested to know the process to treat themselves or others. The description gives the basic idea of treatment of particular zone or organs of the body with their respective colours.

Red Colour : Relates to Root Chakra (*Muladhara*).

Its Location	: Base of spine, perineum.
Concerned Gland	: Adrenal gland.
Concerned Organs	: Legs, Feet, Bones, Large intestine.
Functions	: Survival, Grounding, Life Promoting, Vital Physical Energy.
Malfunction Symptoms	: Constipation Haemorrhoids Obesity Sciatica Arthritis Knee trouble Anorexia Nervosa.

By treating the patient at *muladhara* with red radiation and red radiated oil we can also cure the malfunctioning of human body as stated above and very good results can be obtained without any side effect.

Orange Colour : Relates to Sacral Chakra (*Swadhistan*).

Its Location	: A few inches below navel, lower abdomen, first lumbar vertebra.

Concerned Glands	:	Ovaries, Testicles.
Concerned Organs	:	Uterus, Genitals, Kidney, Bladder, Circulatory System.
Functions	:	Assimilation, Life promoting relating to well-being, Emotions, Sexuality, Immunity from diseases, Desire and Pleasure.
Malfunction Symptoms	:	Kidney/Bladder trouble, Female and male organic, emotional and sexual problems, Lower back problems.

The symptoms described under malfunctioning of body can easily be cured with this coloured radiation and by taking orange water 20–25 ml after every meal.

Yellow Colour : Relates to Solar Plexus Chakra (*Manipura*).

Its Location	:	Eighth thoracic vertebra just below notch where ribs come together to form xyphoid process to navel.
Concerned Glands	:	Pancreas, Adrenals.
Functions	:	Will power, Personal power, Taking in of Energy from outside of self, Growth, Healing.
Malfunction Symptoms	:	Digestive trouble Ulcer Diabetes Hypoglycemia Liver disorder Fat metabolism.

The malfunction symptoms and diseases can be easily cured with this colour without any side effect.

Green Colour : Relates to Heart Chakra (*Anahata*).

Its Location	:	First thoracic vertebra, heart.
Glands	:	Thymus.
Organs	:	Heart, Lungs, Arms, Hands.

Functions	:	Self love and love for others
		Taking in life nourishment in general, mental energy, Consciousness healing.
Malfunctions	:	Heart disease (inclusive high blood pressure) Asthma Lungs diseases.

Although these are very serious diseases, these can be easily cured by drinking green radiated water on empty stomach during morning and evening with application radiations of green colour at the prescribed points. Results are very much fruitful without any side effect.

Sky Blue : Relates to Throat Chakra (*Visudha*).

Its Location	:	Third cervical vertebra.
Related Glands	:	Thyroid and Parathyroid.
Related Organs	:	Neck, Shoulders, Arms, Hands, Ears.
Related Functions	:	Gateway to communication expressive energy, Will (discernment and power of choosing), Synthesizing of symbols into ideals.
Malfunctions	:	Thyroid problem Hearing problem Stiff Neck Colds Sore throats.

Through the application of radiations sky blue colour and intake of the same colour radiated water diseases pointed out in malfunctions can be cured easily without any side effect.

Blue (Royal) : It relates to Brown Chakra (*Ajna*). It is also called the third eye chakra.

Its Location	:	First cervical vertebra in the back (space on forehead slightly above eyes).
Related Gland	:	Pituitary (works in harmony with pineal).
Related Organ	:	Eyes.
Functions	:	Vision, Intuition, Synthesizing.
Malfunctions	:	Headache Vision Problem Nightmares.

With the radiations of Royal Blue colour and intake of the same colour radiated water, diseases pointed out in malfunctions can be cured easily without any side effect.

Violet Colour : Relates to Crown Chakra (*Sahasrara*).

Its Location	:	Top of head and slightly back where soft spot of baby's head is located.
Related Gland	:	Pineal (works in harmony with pituitary).
Related Organs	:	Cerebral Cortex, Central Nervous System.
Functions	:	Integration and understanding, liberation into cosmic realm, bliss.
Malfunctions	:	Depression Alienation Inability to learn or comprehend.

By providing violet radiations at the related points we can very well remove the malfunctions due to pineal gland. There will not be any side effect.

Colour-Radiated Medicines

In this section, different coloured radiated medicines and their usages for different diseases are briefly explained.

Blue-Radiated Materials

Blue Misri : Misri, sugar or milksugar which are radiated for more than 45 days (45 days minimum), can be used for throat problem. (Its dosage is merely 1 gram). As per requirement of patient, generally the dose is given after every 2/3 hours. These dry medicines are very convenient to carry to distant places, instead of bottled liquid contents.

Blue radiated lukewarm water is used for gargles. It is very good for throat and tonsil problems.

Blue Glycerine : If radiated blue glycerine (min. 45 days radiations) is used for toothache and swelling of gums, it gives very positive results.

Blue Water : For any type of stomach infections charged blue water can be used 3 to 4 times a day (dose: 2 to 3 oz, i.e. 25 ml approximately).

Blue Oil : If blue oil is charged at least for 45 days duration and then applied through massage on different parts of the affected body, it can help in healing processes and coping with the problems of headaches and high fever.

If it is massaged over head scalp, the patient will be relieved of headache and feel very comfortable.

If it is massaged over head scalp and forehead, the patient will be relieved of high fevers and headache too.

If a blue (royal) piece of cotton cloth dipped in chilled blue radiated water is applied on the forehead of patient, the high temperature of the body will come down through this process.

Dizziness : Massage of blue oil on scalp of human body and taking the dose of 30–35 ml of blue (royal) charged water (charged for at least 24 hours in 3 days) will help you to get good sound sleep.

For mosquito & scorpion bites : Use the radiated blue oil on affected parts of the body. It will help in relieving the pain and subsequent cure.

For burn : If you get your skin burnt, application of blue charged oil will definitely relieve you of pain and also help you in healing the wound.

Piles : In case you are having piles (without or with bleeding) apply the blue radiated mustard oil inside the orifice with ringfinger. Your piles problems will be cured and you will be relieved of your pain.

The piles patients are advised to keep the stomach always clean of toxic and morbid contents to avoid constipation. They should also avoid the spicy or fried foods as well as sugar containing eatables.

Pimples, Boils, Skin Itching, Eczema and other related skin problems : Use of blue charged radiated (for at least 45 days) glycerine will help you get rid of these problems. In such skin diseases, the patients are advised to get rid of constipation and hormonal disorders. Women in particular should be more cautious because of their delicate body formation and organs. Avoid eatables rich in spices and fats. Avoid sweet dishes. Simple food habits should be adopted with maximum fibrous food.

Ear-ache and problems :	Fully charged/radiated blue oil (for at least 45 days) be heated to a tolerable temperature and may be poured (3 to 4 drops) in both the ears. The ears may be closed with cotton buds and kept at least for 30 minutes duration. This will relieve you from pain. Chronic problems of ears will start healing in a reasonable time.
Restoring Normalcy to Nervous System :	Fully charged/radiated blue oil (at least for 45 days), if massaged over the body, helps in keeping intact the circulatory channels and prevent malfunctioning. The process of massage is to be undertaken regularly on daily basis at least for a month to get the positive results.
	After regular massage for 15 minutes, it is advised to take steam/sauna bath. The results of such process are very stimulating and encouraging.
Teething problem of Infants :	If blue radiated oil is massaged on infant's head, it helps the infants in their teething problems. Application of blue glycerine on gums of infant will also act as catalyst.
Persons involved in lot of Brain Work :	The massage of blue oil regularly on scalp of persons who do a lot of brain work in their daily routine

helps them to contain mental tension and body fatigue.

Note: The blue radiated/charged glycerine/oil can just be applied (not massaged) on sensitive problem zones where they exist i.e. on pimples, boils, eczema and nape of neck etc.

Green-Radiated Medicines

The most valuable contribution of green colour is to get rid of waste and toxic matters from the body. It purifies the blood. It also helps the body to gather extra energy and strength to cope up with the energy consuming acts effectively in daily routine.

Green-Charged Water

After cleaning the green bottles perfectly and carefully, fill them with pure and cleaned water below their necks, so that water inside the bottles may move properly. Seal the bottles, clean their outside surfaces so that dust particles may not be accumulated because these can prevent the inflow of green light radiation, which is required to be absorbed into the water inside the bottles.

This water kept for 3 days is enough to use in emergency cases and after minimum 7 days it attains most properties of green radiations.

For Typhoid Malaria and Measles	:	Green water is used in 20–25 ml quantity for 3 to 4 times a day depending upon the potency required to meet with the patient's problem. Good results are observed. The biggest advantage of taking this green radiated water is to purify blood and increase the vigour.
Tonsils & Fever	:	Generally it has been observed in most of the cases that the patient with tonsil problem gets fever also. When the fever shoots up to level of 102°F, this therapy works wonderfully to combat the fever-related problems.

	If the body temperature of patient is more than 102°F *then he/she should be given blue radiated/charged water to tide over the complications of high fever, accompanied with tonsillitis.*
Soar Throat Cough with Phlegm :	These are the routine problems of human body and can easily be tackled with green radiated water with the dosage of 20–25 ml three to four times a day. Number of dosage can also be increased depending upon the condition of patient and *this can only be learnt from the experience.* In such cases, spicy, chilled and excessive fatty foods or eatables must be avoided.
Eye Diseases & Cure :	Rose water is applied to eyes instead of plain water and it should be radiated/charged for more than 15 days (minimum 15 days). It can be used to treat different eye related problems as indicated below:
Redness in Eyes :	It can be due to extra fatigue, pollution, dust effect or excess heat in the body (stomach). If washed with the charged green water for 3 to 4 times a day, it will act positively. Dosages (3 to 4) of blue radiated water in 20–25 ml quantity be also taken after washing the eyes with rose radiated water.
Cataract and other Eye Problems like Eyesight etc. :	The rose water charged for minimum 15 days be used 3 to 4 times a day for eye washing as

well as in the form of eye drops. This will cure the eye problems and also help to get rid of cataract (initial stage) very effectively.

Regular use of the charged/ radiated rose water will also improve eye sight and prevent ill-effects likely to occur.

Thus it is advised to use green radiated water daily as eye drops to combat any sort of malfunctioning of such an important organ of the body. Neglecting eye problems may lead one to complete blindness.

Stomach : Already elaborated and explained that the green radiated/charged water helps to cure various stomach problems, provided it is charged for at least 15 days.

By consuming regularly 3–4 times a day in the 20–25 ml quantity, it helps the stomach to be safe from infection.

A patient suffering from dysentery should take regularly as per his/her requirement the green water at short intervals. It will definitely improve his/her condition.

If any part of your body is suffering from septic problem, you are advised to clean the septic portion/ wash it with green charged water and take at regular intervals (at least four times a day) to get rid of the problem.

		Regular intake of green-charged water on empty stomach or at the urge of maximum appetite, during morning or evening, helps to ease the chronic constipation problem.
Eczema	:	If your body is having eczema problem, besides application of blue radiated oil, intake of green water will help you a lot in curing the eczema disease. Take it regularly at least 3–4 times (in the prescribed dosage of 20–25 ml) a day on empty stomach (whenever you are at the urge of maximum appetite).
Ring Worms	:	The intake of green radiated water at regular intervals (20–25 ml, 3 to 4 times a day) will help you get rid of ring worms without any side effect.

Above all, regular intake of green charged water helps a lot in controlling/curing:

High blood pressure

Palpitation

It also provides spiritual calmness.

Red Colour-Radiated Medicines

The red colour has the maximum wavelength and is deep penetrating while the violet colour has got the minimum wavelength and less penetration ability. Therefore, the red colour has the maximum heating effect. Because of this, red radiations are used in healing the painful areas of body with maximum heating effects.

Mango, dates, ajwain, garlic are some of the daily consumable items having maximum heat effect in their properties.

Red Oil	: Til oil is kept directly in sun light in red coloured bottles or covered with red cellophane paper from outside and exposed directly to sun light at least for 45 days. Regular dusting of bottles be made from outside so that oil may be charged with red rays properly. The more the bottles kept for radiations, the more their contents become effective. It helps to overcome the problems of various pains, gout and arthritis as well. Apply a little amount of oil on the affected area and rub it slowly to get it absorbed into the body. Then red radiations are given from red light for at least 10 to 15 minutes. Day by day you will start getting relief.
Paralysis Problem	: Red oil is also very effective in case of paralytic patients. Apply and absorb the red oil on paralytic portions and complete anterior and posterior trunk portions. Deep penetrated red radiations are also to be given. The results thus seen are very positive and patient starts improving miraculously.
Pain due to Cold	: If a patient is suddenly suffering from cough and cold, his or her whole body starts paining. In such cases, rubbing of red oil on portions where the patient is feeling *congestion* due to cold, provides immediate relief and the recovery is remarkable.

Ears : If any patient is having pus problem in the ear or is hard of hearing, then lukewarm red oil, prepared by at least 45 days radiations, be poured into the affected ear. Red radiations may also be given. Patient will start improving day by day.

Chronic diseases, like *cough, asthma, pneumonia* can also be treated successfully with the red oil massage on anterior and posterior trunk portions, especially on the chest. Red radiations are also given. Remarkable results are seen in such cases and patients get very much satisfaction after being relieved of disease.

Cracks of heels during winter are cured by application of red radiated oil. It is sufficient to cope up with such itching and pain problem.

If you are prone to joints pain, waist pain, pain in the neck, then red oil massage and red radiation is the only solution to get rid of your problem. Methods of preparation and application of oil have already been explained earlier.

Red oil application and its massage act as an agent in curing impotency.

Method of preparation of red oil and its use for massage are similar to that of other diseases. These have already been explained in earlier pages.

Orange Colour & Its Properties

Orange colour is related to Sacral Chakra (*Swadhistan*) and its pivoted place is two to three inches below the navel (Umbilicus). It is the master of lower abdomen. The glands covered and controlled are *ovaries* and *testes*. The complementary organs dependent are *uterus, genitals, kidney, bladder* and *body circulatory system*. The functioning system controls *assimilation, life promoting, emotions, sexuality, desire* and *pleasure*. Due to its deficiency, *kidney/bladder troubles* occur. *Female/Male organic emotional and sexual problems* arise. Among all, the *lower back problems* are the main ones.

The Process : Take brown beer bottles, wash them properly to get rid of any infection and dry them. Now fill them with fresh water upto 2/3rd of the bottles (for proper movement of the liquid) and seal it. Keep the bottles exposed to sun light for its radiations to charge the water with orange colour. These bottles are to be cleaned from outside and shaken everyday for at least 3 days or maximum up to 7 days to get your medicine prepared.

The charged water has properties of orange colour. As it is very good for digestion, it can be taken 20–25 ml dosage after meals. This will improve your digestion system and metabolism. You can use it as a regular tonic.

It will help in curing your *gastric* problems, rejuvenate your red blood cells and give new lives to them to carry oxygen to different parts of your body. *If red blood cells are sound and strong enough in their functioning, you will feel very active all the time.*

It is very beneficial in all types of cough problems if taken regulary after the meals in 20–25 ml dosage per intake.

It is most effective and beneficial to regulate proper blood circulation in the body in order to rejuvenate the R.B.Cs. Therefore, the problems related to improper circulation which generate diseases like *gouts* and *gathia* can be kept away through its regular use, i.e. half a cup twice or thrice a day.

Caution : High blood pressure patients should not use this therapy.

Vocal Cord Paralysis can also be cured by regular usage of orange water twice or thrice a day with half a cup as dosage.

It is also very effective in *bed-wetting problems* of infants. Precaution regarding infant dosage is always to be taken. Dosage for infants is just half the dosage of adults.

On the whole, to maintain best circulatory system, orange water is the best tonic if used in prescribed dosages for adults and infants regularly.

Orthodox View—A Caution

Although colour therapists will treat any disorder, be it mental, emotional, metabolic or physical, still they emphasise that their therapy is complementary to qualified medical treatment, not exactly an alternative to it. Patients, therefore, should always seek the advice of their orthodox doctors as well.

The work of colour therapists is not regarded as harmful.

A Treatise on Home Remedies

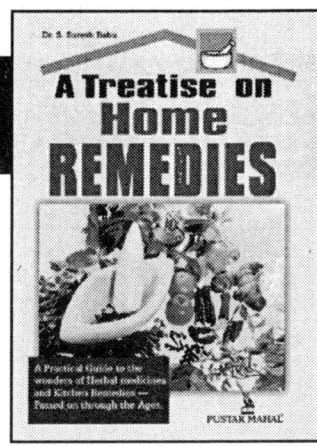

—*Dr. S. Suresh Babu, M.D. (Ayur)*

A practical guide to the wonders of Herbal medicines and Kitchen remedies—passed on through the Ages.

Modern medical science may be effective in treating a variety of diseases, but often fails when it comes to chronic problems like gastric-disorders, common cold, respiratory ailments and many others. Here the positive role of traditional, ayurvedic and herbal and home medicines has been proven beyond doubt.

This volume brings you an overview of specific problems—backed by not only ayurvedic remedies but also home remedies, along with dietary restrictions and do's & don'ts. From flatulence, constipation, cirrhosis of liver to hepatitis, jaundice and common cold—it covers a broad range. For instance, how a peptic ulcer is formed, and how cold milk is useful in providing relief. Or what are the problems accompanying dysentery and how the 'Bel' fruit is effective in its treatment.

The unique feature of the book is the treatment through Home Remedies—items which we've always had at hand in our kitchen like haldi, methi, coconut, cumin (jeera), clove, castor etc. What's more—additional treatments in the form of medicated massages, Hydrotherapy through fomentation methods and Home Beauty aids also bring you useful tips for a healthy and happy life.

Big Size • Pages: 220
Price: Rs. 150/- • Postage: Rs.15/-

75 HEALTH CHARTS

—*M.K. Gupta*

As any health-conscious person knows, health is truly wealth. Yet, simply harbouring good intentions does not ensure good health for anyone. Beginning in infancy and right up to our twilight years, a conscious attempt has to be made to lead a healthy lifestyle. In the formative years, our parents make this effort on our behalf. But as we enter the teens and take control of our own destinies, how well informed we are on health-related issues makes all the difference between physical well-being and ill health.

This book ensures you have all the facts, figures and data at your fingertips to promote proper health and nutrition in order to prevent disease. Indeed, the cost of prevention is a pittance compared to the cost of a cure. Towards this end, *75 Health Charts* has it all: height and weight charts, blood pressure and pulse rate charts, calorie charts, fat and cholesterol charts, vitamin and mineral charts, balanced diet charts, pollution health hazard charts, infectious diseases and immunisation charts, healthy heart and stress charts... not to mention other relevant charts, tables and data.

So, if health has always been your problem, this book is just what the doctor ordered. And if health has been your forte, this book is exactly what the doctor would recommend to maintain you in the pink of your health. Either way, *75 Health Charts* is a must-read for all people.

Big Size • Pages: 144
Price: Rs. 120/- • Postage: Rs. 15/-

Alternative Therapy

Magic Therapy of Colours

—*A.R. Hari*

Holistic healing through colours

In vogue since ancient times, colour therapy has now come of age as a holistic method of treatment. Global research justifies the application of colour in many disorders. Administered by a trained practitioner, colour therapy is safe, complementary to other systems and relatively inexpensive in India.

Modern man spends most of his life cooped up within homes and offices or automobiles. Thanks to the odd hours they keep, some people even spend a few months without being exposed to sunlight. The body and mind are casualties when we miss out on the invigorating colour vibrations present in nature. The good health of the ancients was partly because they allowed all colours in nature to energise their bodies by being outdoors during the day. Having a proper balance of healthy colours in the interiors of our homes and offices can partly rectify this shortcoming.

The Magic Therapy of Colours outlines the history of colour therapy, modern methods of utilising colour and the areas it is beneficial in. The book is an invaluable guide for those seeking holistic benefits from colour therapy.

Demy Size • Pages: 119
Price: Rs. 80/- • Postage: Rs. 15/-

Alternative Therapy

Fruit and Vegetable Juice Therapy

—*Dr. Syed Aziz Ahmad & Dr. S.C. Sharma*

Curative & preventive properties of fruits & vegetables in ensuring a healthy body & glowing skin

Did you know that papaya, orange, lemon and pomegranate act as antidotes to high blood pressure... or *amla* and carrot are useful in controlling asthma... or guava and *mosambi* help in regulating constipation? In fact, each and every fruit and vegetable has incredible curative properties, and offers a natural way to good health. Fruits and vegetables act as scavengers to our body, and drive away toxic and harmful wastes. They nourish our body with pure water, sugar, vitamins, minerals, proteins, fibres, aromatic compounds and a host of other micro-nutrients. Grab this authentic, self-help, therapeutic guide to learn and apply the remarkable ways to combat naturally all kinds of ailments. Some examples—

- ❖ High B.P. antidotes: Papaya, orange, lemon, pomegranate.
- ❖ Skin disease preventives: Apple, carrot, watermelon, lemon.
- ❖ Asthma prophylactics: *Amla*, carrot, pomegranate.
- ❖ Fever combatants: Orange, *mosambi*, pomegranate.
- ❖ Diarrhoea curatives: Pineapple, apple, pomegranate.
- ❖ Constipation regulators: Guava, *mosambi*, apple.
- ❖ Digestion aid: Spinach (*palak*).
- ❖ Diabetic control: Bitter gourd (*karela*).
- ❖ Jaundice & Diarrhoea control: Carrot.

Demy Size • Pages: 218
Price: Rs. 96/- • Postage: Rs. 15/-

Alternative Therapy

The Magic of AROMATHERAPY

—Gwydion O'Hara

"A wonderful introduction for beginners in aromatherapy as well as a quick reference guide for experienced practitioners. This is the first book ever that I have seen which gives both the healing properties of herbs and their magical properties. Excellent."
—Reverend Ray T. Malbrough
Charms, Spells & Formulas

Breathe in the Magic

Breathe in the intoxicating aroma of lavender, orange and pine to relieve stress. Attract unconditional love by sprinkling rose, jasmine, carnation and apple into a steaming bath. From therapeutic applications for massage, pain relief, and mental clarity to magical applications for love, prosperity, and ritual, the 332 recipes in *The Magic of Aromatherapy* will help you balance your physical, mental, and spiritual selves.

But you'll get more than just recipes in this unusually complete guide. You'll learn the 'why' of essential oils—traditional, historical and cultural uses—plus you get an exhaustive reference section with planetary, astrological, elemental and gender associations; magical and therapeutic properties; magical cross-references; and a listing of oil sources.

Demy Size • Pages: 264
Price: Rs. 135/- • Postage: Rs. 15/-

Alternative Therapy

The Miracle of
Music Therapy
—*Rajendar Menen*

Music is all around us. It marks every event of our life, from birth, marriage and death to the phases in-between. Man has long known that music has the ability to calm, cajole and rejuvenate. But it is only recently that science has begun to understand, study and document the effects of music in methodology, which leaves little room for doubt.

It is now an established fact that music helps all living creatures—from plants to birds and animals and man—to grow and rejuvenate. Music permeates the cells of all living beings, alters mood swings, cell division, heals the ailing, induces sleep, creates wakefulness, and dances with the mood, the mind and the soul.

While the *rishis* of ancient India and the Vedas first documented the effects of music on the human beings and all living things, it was left to the western world to fashion the more modern concepts of healing through music. There are now serious music therapy courses in the world's best universities and remunerative openings abroad for music therapists. This book dwells heavily on the findings from ancient India and the masters of today who have made music therapy a viable healing alternative. It is the most comprehensive guide on the healing powers of sound and music.

Demy Size • Pages: 144
Price: Rs. 80/- • Postage: Rs. 15/-

The Acupressure Handbook

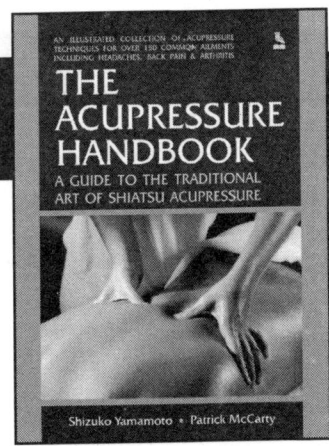

—*Shizuko Yamamoto*
& Patrick McCarty

A guide to the traditional art of Shiatsu Acupressure

This unique book is a comprehensive collection of acupressure techniques and natural healing remedies designed to bring about immediate relief from a variety of pains and illnesses. Using easy-to-follow instructions and numerous photographs and illustrations, this book guides you through the various applications of *Shiatsu* massage.

This book is divided into three sections. Section I, *Foundation*, provides a history of *Shiatsu* along with that of macrobiotics. It examines the root causes of illness as well as fundamental principles of the natural forces that affect us all. It shows you how you can draw upon the healing process within each of us. Section II explains how to give a complete *Shiatsu*-acupressure treatment—including the loosening phase, designed to increase circulation and relax the body, and the whole body phase, the pressing and massaging of the neck, shoulders, back, abdomen and arms. A discussion of the various touching techniques is also included. Section III shows you specific acupressure techniques for over 150 common ailments, including allergies, arthritis, asthma, colds, fatigue, hay fever, headaches, high blood pressure, sciatica and more. Throughout the book, the authors provide insights, advice, and practical tips based upon their own years of experience.

Big Size • *Pages: 264*
Price: Rs. 150/- • *Postage: Rs. 25/-*

Alternative Therapy

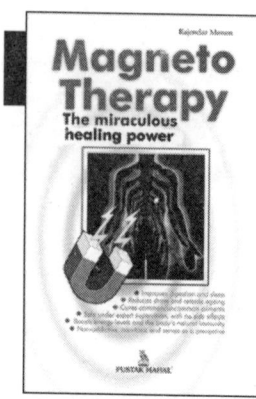

Magneto-Therapy
The miraculous healing power

—*Rajendar Menen*

Be it an ailment that has you at your wits' end or the fact that you simply seek to enhance your general well-being without burning a hole in your pocket or suffering unforeseen side effects, magneto-therapy is just the right choice for you.

The book is divided into two sections. Section I focuses on magnets, magnetism and magneto-therapy in general and its status in India, while Section II deals with the scenario in the West regarding research, treatments and advances in magneto-therapy. From the origins of magneto-therapy to its current status, from everyday cures to the larger influence of magnets on our lives, from products that are easily available to experiments conducted with magnets all over the world on human, plant and animal life, you will find all this and much more in the book.

If practised properly and diligently, before long, you should be eating well, sleeping well and feeling a general sense of well-being at all times.

Demy Size • Pages: 128
Price: Rs. 108/- Postage: Rs. 15/-

Alternative Therapy

WATER
A Miracle Therapy
—*A.R. Hari*

The more science has advanced, the further away have we moved from Mother Nature. Thanks to our artificial existence, even to quench a natural urge like thirst, we imbibe synthetic substances such as colas and caffeine-loaded drinks.

Having starved our body of Nature's most precious liquid, water, we are beset with multiple ailments like headaches, arthritis, asthma, urinary problems, general debility, blood pressure and the like. Missing the root cause of the problem, we rush to doctors—only to have antibiotics pumped into us that offer short-term "relief" while turning into long-term nightmares.

This book shows how drinking just 12 to 14 glasses of water per day (for the average person) cures many ailments, including chronic ones. Incredibly, by just carefully following the 'Water Protocol' in the book, you may feel the difference within 48 hours! Just like a water-starved house plant that springs to attention within minutes of being watered.

Demy Size • Pages: 112
Price: Rs. 80/- • Postage: Rs. 15/-

The Practical
Book of REIKI
—*Mrs. Rashmi Sharma &*
Maharaj Krishan Sharma
Healing Through
Universal Lifeforce Energy

Find balance and harmony in the mind and spirit. It is truly a gift to yourself! Increase your vibratory level and healing capacity by treating yourself and others. Be sure to engage your intuitive knowledge, feel free so that you can maintain the accelerated ability to channel the Reiki energy. Remove the energy blocks and negative thoughts from Chakras and personality traits.

Apply Reiki by following the five principles:
- ❖ Just for today I will live with attitude of gratitude
- ❖ Just for today I will not worry
- ❖ Just for today I will not be angry
- ❖ Just for today I will do my work honestly
- ❖ Just for today I will show love and respect for every living thing.

This unique book is for those who are looking for a useful treatise for self-treatment and transformation with the principles of Reiki.

Big Size • Pages: 168
Price: Rs. 108/- • Postage: Rs. 15/-